From A to Z: Teaching Skills to Children with Autism

A collection of simple, successful strategies to teach academic, self-help, and social skills to children with Autism using Applied Behavior Analysis techniques

Acknowledgments

This book was a labor of love, and my wish is that it gives encouragement, creative ideas, and support to everyone who reads it. Autism is multi-faceted and impacts every individual differently. If Autism is multi-dimensional and complex, then the strategies or treatments to teach a child with Autism must be multi-dimensional as well. Every child deserves a teacher who believes the child can be successful. I hope that this book empowers you to believe in the potential of every child with Autism that you encounter.

"I am not a teacher, but an awakener" Robert Frost, 1874-1963

From A to Z!

Introduction

Children with Autism often exhibit deficits in a variety of different areas, including academics, language, social skills, and self help skills. In order to interact with people and the environment in a meaningful way, it is vital that children with Autism learn to overcome these deficits to the best of their ability. Some children with Autism can learn to eventually overcome their individual deficits, while some children with Autism will always need some degree of assistance due to the deficits that affect them. My opinion is that the #1 goal of Applied Behavior Analysis is to make as much progress as possible, across as many deficit areas as possible. This book you are holding in your hands will help you reduce or eliminate deficits that are impeding learning or social functioning in the life of a child with Autism. "From A to Z" includes a variety of specific skills, both complex and simple, beginning with learning adjectives and ending with learning to use a zipper.

There are often hundreds of ways to teach any specific skill and this book is a collection of practical Applied Behavior Analysis strategies that anyone can implement. What do I mean by "anyone"? Well….anyone!

Teachers, speech therapists, ABA therapists, babysitters, parents, tutors, nannies, grandparents, siblings, social workers, and anyone else who cares for a child with Autism, and wants to help them learn.

From A to Z!

Teaching children with Autism can be such a satisfying and creative process once you determine the best way to reach the particular child. I hope that the strategies in this book are successful for you, get your creativity flowing, and most importantly show how diverse successful teaching strategies can be.

I largely minimize the use of technical language to make the concepts described easier to understand. However if you come across a specific ABA term that you aren't familiar with you can quickly flip to the glossary in the back of the book for a list of common ABA terms and definitions. I want you to have full understanding as you are reading the strategies and techniques described in this book.

The skills described in this book are intended to be appropriate for children with Autism of varying functioning levels between the ages of 2-8. Some of the skills listed are more appropriate for higher functioning children who are vocal, and some of the activities can be successful with lower functioning children who do not talk. Each skill has a clear goal, suggested materials, a specific activity, and easy generalization tips.

There are many ABA teaching tools and helpful tips listed throughout this book, as well as helpful resources in the back of the book for any ABA program. Whether you are a professional or a parent, this book is intended to empower you to modify instruction to teach skills to children with Autism. If you know a child with Autism who is having difficulties learning it may not be the teacher or student who is to blame; simple modifications to the curriculum could

From A to Z!

solve the problem. This book is intended to empower you to know how to make such modifications and to generalize your teaching strategies.

Learning doesn't just occur in classrooms; it happens all day long across many environments. Thusly, all of us are "teachers" of someone.

Good luck teachers, and have fun!

From A to Z

Adjectives
Goal: The child will understand the concept of adjectives.
Materials: Colorful balls of varying size from tiny to large
*Tip: It will be easier to teach the child to understand adjectives if you begin with items that are clearly very different, such as a golf ball and a beach ball.
Teaching Strategy: Take the child outside and practice throwing balls against the house. Place a very small and very big ball in front of the child, and say "Throw the big ball at the house". Repeat with the small ball. After the child has thrown the ball, bring both balls over to them and have them touch the small ball, and then the big ball. Use prompting as needed to help the child be successful.
Generalization: Go to a park and tell the child you will push them on the big swing, or tell them to bring you a little flower. Use prompting to help the child understand.
Why is this important? Adjectives help children understand categories (big/small, tall/short, etc), and classification.

Animal Sounds
Goal: The child will be able to identify an animal by the sound it makes.
Materials: Picture book with various animals
*Tip: If the child has any pets, start teaching on that specific animal. For example, if the child has a pet kitten then begin animal sounds by teaching the child that a cat says "meow".

From A to Z!

7
Link the lesson to the actual pet that the child has, to make the concept more memorable.
Teaching Strategy: Read the book to the child regularly, and have them point to specific animals. Once the child can identify the animals by touch correctly, begin identifying them by the sound they make: "Point to the one who meows. Good job, the cat meows!" or "Woof woof! Touch the animal that sounds like that".
Generalization: Take the child to a zoo, where they can see a variety of animals. Point out animals and identify them by the sound they make instead of their name. Say to the child "There's the animal that roars! What's his name"?

Why is this important? Knowing animal sounds is part of interacting successfully with the environment, and learning about various animals.

Bathing
Goal: The child will independently bathe themselves.
*Tip: It is often easier to work on bathing skills in the shower versus a bath. Baths can be very relaxing and soothing to children, which while a good thing, can lead to the child just laying in the tub and not actually bathing themselves. Standing in a shower versus sitting down in a tub can often help the child participate in bathing, rather than passively sitting while someone else bathes them.
Materials: Brightly colored shower gel, handheld shower nozzle
Teaching Strategy: Purchase a brightly colored shower gel (if you can find a scented one with a fragrance the child loves, even better) and let the child apply the shower gel to their

body. The colored gel should be clearly visible when placed on the skin. For some children it helps to count as the child applies the gel, to avoid putting a dab of gel on their skin. Squirt some gel in the child's hand or onto their washcloth, and count to 3 as they scrub the gel in. Repeat for various body parts. After the child is soapy, they should use the shower nozzle to wash the gel off their skin, one body part at a time, until the colored gel is no longer visible.

Generalization: Generalize this skill by implementing hygiene checks. One such strategy is called the "5 point check" The child should wash themselves in the shower, and at specific intervals (such as every 15 seconds) the child must stick out of the shower their head, arms, and legs, to show you that each body part has been washed. This is a great way to gradually remove your assistance from the bathing process, as you would just need to walk into the bathroom during each time interval to check the specific body part.

Why is this important? Bathing is a self help skill, which will help the child to be more independent.

Body Parts
Goal: The child will be able to identify their own body parts by touch.
Materials: A life-size drawing of the child
Teaching Strategy: Have the child stand against butcher paper taped to the wall. Trace the child's outline using a marker. Cut out the outline and decorate it to add a face, clothing, and hair. Tape the drawing onto the wall. Have the child stand in front of the drawing as you point to various body parts. Then ask the child to touch the same body part on their body: "This is her nose. Touch your nose".

From A to Z!

9

Generalization: Sing the song "Head, Shoulders, Knees, and Toes" with the child, and help them touch the correct body parts as the song names them.

Why is this important? Children need to know their body parts in order to be aware of the human body.

Blow Bubbles

Goal: The child will be able to blow through a bubble wand to produce bubbles.

Materials: Gum, container of bubbles (with wand)

Teaching Strategy: Allow the child to chew bubblegum, and then practice blowing the gum forcefully out of the mouth. Squeeze the child's cheeks if necessary to help them achieve success with blowing, or model for them with your own gum. It's easier to learn to blow by first blowing something *out of* your mouth. Sit directly in front of the child and say "Do This" as you blow bubbles through a bubble wand. Encourage the child to watch your mouth as you blow.

Generalization: Start teaching blowing with a bubble wand by using a large sized wand that is easier to blow, and eventually using a regular sized wand. Vary the size of the bubble wand that you give to the child, so they learn to blow with light force and with heavy force.

Why is this important? Blowing is an oral-motor activity that can help strengthen muscles in the face, mouth, and jaw.

From A to Z!

Carrier Phrases
Goal: The child will use full sentences to respond to a question.
Materials: "I want" sentence strip, toy or candy the child really likes
Teaching Strategy: Hold up the toy or candy where the child can clearly see it. When the child begins to grab at, reach for, or demand the item, hold up the sentence strip and prompt the child to say "I want (name of item)". Only give the child the item if they say the full sentence.
Generalization: Teach the child a variety of carrier phrases by giving them the answer before you ask the question. Go for a walk down the street, and stop next to a mailbox. Say to the child: "I see a mailbox. What do you see"? The child should respond "I see a mailbox". Eventually, drop the first statement and just ask "What do you see"?

Why is this important? In order to speak in complete sentences with proper grammar, children need to know a variety of carrier phrases.

Catch a Ball
Goal: The child will be able to catch a ball that is thrown to them
Materials: Medium sized lightweight balls (less risk of injury while the child is learning to catch)
Teaching Strategy: Sit on the floor facing the child and practice tossing a ball back and forth. If possible, have another person sit behind the child to put their arms in the correct position to catch. The child should extend both arms, with palms facing up. As the child begins learning the skill, back up to 1 foot, 2

From A to Z!

feet, etc., until the child can stand 5-7 feet away and catch the ball.

Generalization: Play a game that involves catching, such as baseball or football. Don't use the traditional balls for the sport. Play football with a beach ball, or play baseball with a tennis ball. This makes the game more fun for the child, while also getting them comfortable with catching a variety of different balls.

Why is this important? Ball play is a fun physical activity, and also can lead to play interactions with peers.

Category Sorting

Goal: The child will be able to demonstrate understanding of categories of objects or items.

Materials: Laundry consisting of pieces of identical clothing, non identical clothing, and 1-3 non clothing items (such as a fork, book, and pen)

Teaching Strategy: Place a laundry basket full of laundry in front of the child for the child to sort. When initially teaching sorting, the items in the basket should be very different: e.g. 2 identical red shirts and a book. This makes it very easy for the child to discriminate between what goes together and what does not. As the child begins to learn the skill, increase the difficulty level. Place similar, but different, items in the laundry basket such as 2 red shirts, 2 pink shirts, and 2 red socks. At this point you can also have the child sort by a specific category, by saying to the child "sort socks" or "sort red".

Generalization: To help generalize the skill of sorting into categories, you can have the child sort items out group by group. Have the child help you clear the dining room table

From A to Z!

after a meal, and ask for groupings of items one at a time: 'Bring me the forks", "Bring me the plates", "Bring me the cups", etc. Depending on the functioning level of the child you may need to use pictures or prompting to help them complete the task.

> *Why is this important?* Categorization leads to understanding systems of classification, and why items are similar or dissimilar.

Community Helpers

Goal: The child will be able to identify a variety of common professions and people relevant to their community based on specific characteristics, such as recognizing someone is a chef because they wear a big white chef's hat, a white jacket, and are holding a spatula.

Materials: 4-6 flashcards of common community helpers (teacher, police officer, doctor, etc.), and 4-6 flashcards of equipment associated with each profession (chalkboard, police car, stethoscope, etc)

Teaching Strategy: Have the child match the equipment to the profession that uses it. Simplify this task by giving the child only one choice: present a flashcard with a police officer on it, and put a flashcard with a police car in front of the child. Tell the child to "match". As the child begins to learn the skill, increase the difficulty by adding more flashcards to choose from.

Generalization: Engage in a game of pretend play with the child using costumes/clothing, such as dressing up as a fireman. Place a fireman's hat and a police officers hat in front of the child and ask them to give you the hat a fireman would wear. Make the game fun and playful and encourage the child to "act out" each profession, such as pretending to put out a fire while wearing the fireman's hat.

> *Why is this important?* Community Helpers is intended to teach the child about the people in their environment and community.

Cooking

Goal: The child will be able to prepare a simple meal.
Materials: Visual recipe, any necessary utensils or food items
Teaching Strategy: A visual recipe is a way of making a recipe easy to understand by using photos instead of words. This is a great way to begin to teach a child to cook, and for a child with Autism, the visuals help aid understanding. Start with a simple dish that doesn't require the use of a stove or microwave, such as a sandwich. Have someone take photos of you as you prepare a sandwich. For example, step 1: photo of bread, step 2: photo of peanut butter and jelly, step 3: photo of a butter knife, etc. Have a photo for each step of the process. Bring the child into the kitchen and tell them its time to cook (to make this skill less difficult, have the necessary items and materials lined up on the counter). If the child has an understanding of sequencing, you can line the photos up in order and direct the child through each step. If the child does not understand sequencing, simply hand the child each photo one at a time. Prompt the child to look at the photo, and then complete the step "First, you need bread. Get the bread." Continue prompting the child through each step as necessary, until they have completed the recipe.
Generalization: Generalize this skill by creating varied visual recipes, such as for drinks, desserts, snacks, breakfast foods, etc. As the child learns the skill and becomes more capable,

include simple recipes that require the use of the microwave or stove.

> *Why is this important?* Cooking is a self help skill, which will help the child to become more independent.

Dressing Skills
Goal: The child will be able to independently dress themselves, or undress themselves.
Materials: A large doll (life sized, if you can find one) or stuffed animal, and various articles of clothing
Teaching Strategy: Practice placing clothing onto a large stuffed animal, or a life sized doll. Give the child some control over the activity by letting them choose what to put on the doll. Lay out 2-3 articles of clothing and ask the child "What should (doll's name) wear today"? It may be easier for the child to learn how to dress themselves if they dress a doll or stuffed animal first. Use verbal prompting to remind the child of the steps, such as "Pull the pants all the way up, and then zip the zipper".
Generalization: Transfer this skill to the child by having the child put on an article of clothing as they watch you dress the doll. If the child makes an error getting dressed (doesn't put their shirt on correctly), model the correct way on the doll (e.g. "Put your shirt on like this.").

> *Why is this important?* Dressing is a self help skill, which will help the child to become more independent.

From A to Z!

Drawing
Goal: The child will be able to draw various lines or shapes.
Materials: Various household objects of different shapes, paper.
*Tip: Learning to trace can help children with Autism learn how to draw. Some children do not even scribble on paper, and if given a crayon/marker and paper they won't know what to do with these objects.
Teaching Strategy: Choose items around the home that the child likes or is interested in such as the remote, a cell phone, or a picture book. Have the child trace or outline the object on a piece of paper using a crayon or marker. Once the outline is finished, have the child color in the tracing.
Generalization: After the child has had practice tracing an object a few times, make this task more difficult by having the child draw the object. For example, place a book in front of the child and tell the child "Draw book". Provide assistance as needed to help the child with proper grip and attending to the object. Use repetition to strengthen this skill.

> *Why is this important?* Drawing is a prerequisite to writing, which is an important school readiness skill.

Emotions
Goal: The child will be able to identify common emotions both receptively and expressively.
Materials: Flashcards depicting various emotions (happy, angry, scared, etc.)
Teaching Strategy: Help the child receptively identify emotions by holding up a flashcard and telling them to

From A to Z!

16

"Touch happy" (or whichever emotion is being portrayed). As the child learns the flashcards, add in 1 more card and see if the child can discriminate between cards. Increase the difficulty of the skill by having the child touch the correct card, and then hold up the card and say "How does he/she feel"?

Generalization: Flip through a magazine with the child, and point to different facial expressions. Alternate between labeling the emotions portrayed for the child ("Oh, she feels happy! She's smiling") and asking the child how the person in the magazine feels. If this task seems too difficult for the child, offer them a choice of emotions "Does he feel mad or scared"?

Why is this important? Understanding emotions is important for regulating one's own emotional needs, as well as reacting appropriately to the emotional needs of others.

Eye Contact

Goal: The child will be able to make and sustain appropriate eye contact.
Materials: Small stickers
*Tip: Eye contact can be very difficult for children with Autism, and even after being taught to make eye contact some children will prefer to look just above, just below, or just to the side of your eyes and not directly into your eyes. Sustaining eye contact can also be difficult for children with Autism, and they may prefer to make brief eye contact and then look away.
Teaching Strategy: Place a small sticker on your forehead. Engage the child in conversation, or ask them a question. Prompt the child to look at you by pointing to the sticker on your forehead and saying "Look". The sticker helps motivate the child to look at you. Over time, you can move the sticker

From A to Z!

closer and closer to your eyes, and then remove the sticker completely until the child is looking at you appropriately. Generalization: Make a game of eye contact by placing the sticker on various body parts. Place the sticker on your hand, knee, elbow, etc., and each time point to the sticker and tell the child "Look"! Be sure to give excited and fun praise to the child each time they follow the sticker with their eye gaze, such as tickles or high fives.

Why is this important? Eye contact is an important skill for socialization and peer interaction, and eye contact also helps with attending to others in a classroom setting.

Emotional Regulation
Goal: The child will be able to identify their own emotions, and self-manage their emotions appropriately.
*Tip: This skill is particularly helpful for older children (6 and up) who are prone to mood swings or sudden fits of anger. A typical child with Autism can have many behavioral triggers throughout the day, that lead to frustration, anger, annoyance, or sometimes a full meltdown. Teaching the child that they are responsible for their own feelings and their own mood can help the child learn self control and appropriate outlets for anger.
Materials: Behavior thermometer, calming music or nature sounds (optional)
Teaching Strategy: Create a behavior thermometer visual by drawing a picture of a thermometer. Label the thermometer with various emotional states, such as "Angry" (color this section red, or label it with a number)", "Happy" (color this section yellow, or label it with a number), etc. The thermometer should be labeled at the top with anger and at

From A to Z!

the bottom with happy, and you can place other emotions in between (depending on the emotional states exhibited by that particular child). The goal is for the child to stay at or near the bottom of the thermometer, in the "happy" range. For younger children photos of facial expressions may be more helpful, while older children might be able to use just words. Teach the child to use the behavior thermometer by explaining each emotional state to them and what it might look or feel like. For example, "When you feel angry you scrunch up your face like this (make a face at the child), and you clench your fists and talk very loudly. Inside (touch the child's stomach) you might feel hot or all tangled up." Help the child label their emotions by telling them when they appear to be upset or calm, such as "You look happy, because you are smiling. Do you feel happy?", as you point to the behavior thermometer. It may take repeated practice to help the child understand the emotions they are feeling, and to express that (receptively or expressively). Schedule "check-in" times during the day where you take the child to the behavior thermometer and have them identify how they are feeling. If the child identifies the wrong feeling, correct them and explain why, such as "You pointed to "happy", but you're crying because your brother took your toy. I think you feel "sad". When the child begins to "climb up" the behavior thermometer, immediately do a check-in and help the child label their emotion. Then direct the child to engage in calming exercises, such as deep breathing and visualization: Take the child to a darkened, quiet room and play calming music at a low level (this is optional, some children don't enjoy calming music). Teach the child to breathe deeply several times in a row, and practice clenching and then unclenching their muscles. As the child learns the skill, begin to remove yourself

From A to Z!

from this process gradually until the child is checking in and doing relaxation exercises independently.

Generalization: Generalize this skill by practicing the steps involved as part of the daily routine. During the "check-in", take a few moments to have the child show you what each emotion looks like. Ask the child "Show me happy", or "Show me sad". Have the child identify the triggers that lead to each emotional state, such as "When I told you it was time for a bath, you got angry." Write down "bath time" on the thermometer near the "angry" section. Identifying triggers for each emotional state will help both the child and caregivers to anticipate mood fluctuations. The goal is not to prevent the child from having mood swings throughout the day, but to teach them an appropriate way to identify and respond to their emotional state.

> *Why is this important?* Understanding emotions is important for regulating one's own emotional needs (i.e. self-control), as well as reacting appropriately to the emotional needs of others.

Fill in the missing word/words

Goal: The child will be able to express understanding and knowledge of various pieces of information, which is a building block for conversation.

Materials: Photos of a recent birthday party

Teaching Strategy: Sit down with the child and direct them to look at photos from a birthday party they attended recently. As you look at the photos together, ask the child about what happened at the party. For example, say to the child "We went to a birthday party on Saturday, and we ate _____", as you point to a photo of the birthday cake. If the child is unable to

expressively fill in the blank, see if they can fill in the blank by pointing to the correct object in the photo. Make this skill more difficult by giving the child fill in the blank questions with no visual stimuli present. For example, say to the child "We went to a birthday party on Saturday, and we ate ____". If the child does not fill in the blank and say "cake", you can prompt the child by whispering in their ear "cake". The child should then repeat after you and answer "cake".
Generalization: Practice fill in the word activities while an activity is actually occurring. Take your child to the park and begin to push them on the swing. Stop the swing, gain eye contact with the child and say to them "You are swinging on a ____". Provide praise if the child responds "swing", and prompting if they do not.

Why is this important? Fill in the blanks are pre-requisites to advanced language skills, such as maintaining a conversation.

Fine Motor Skills
Goal: The child will be able to demonstrate age appropriate fine motor skills.
Materials: Any "O" shaped cereal or candy, string
*Tip: Arts & Crafts are a good way to strengthen fine motor skills, as many children with Autism find the tactile (touch) and visual (sight) stimulation of arts and crafts to be reinforcing and enjoyable.
Teaching Strategy: Help the child make cereal or candy necklaces by giving them string and a few pieces of candy or cereal at a time. Help the child pick up each piece of candy or cereal, and then place it onto the string. Depending on the child, this could be a very difficult activity. Embed

From A to Z!

reinforcement into the task by telling the child that when the necklace is done, they can eat it!

Generalization: Generalize this skill by having the child help you clean up the activity once you are finished. *"Accidentally"* (oops!) drop some of the candy or cereal onto the floor, and have the child help you pick them up and place them back into the container. If the child has fine motor difficulties, they may try to pick up the candy or cereal using a scooping motion with their entire hand. Avoid letting the child do this. Instead model for the child that you want them to pick up the cereal or candy using a pincer grip.

Why is this important? Fine motor skills are necessary to correctly manipulate a variety of items and stimuli in the environment. Fine motor refers to small muscle group actions, such as using a pincer grip, pulling a zipper up, or touching the pinkie to the thumb.

Function, Feature, Class (FFC)
Goal: The child will be able to describe a person, place, or thing by stating the function, feature, and class.
Materials: Stuffed animal that makes sounds, and a non animal toy
Teaching Strategy: Engage in play with the child. Place the stuffed animal and other toy next to each other and ask the child for the stuffed animal based on its function, feature, or class. For example, "Give me the one that barks", "Give me the one with a tail", or "Give me the animal". Make this skill more difficult by holding up the stuffed animal and asking the child to pint out various features, such as "Point to the dog's tail". After the child points to the tail, reinforce their response by saying "That's right! A dog has a tail".

From A to Z!

Generalization: Generalize this skill by using actual objects or people. If you are out with the child and see a dog walking by, point to the dog and say "There's a white doggie! Tell me something a dog has".

> *Why is this important?* FFC's are pre-requisites to advanced language skills, as they help teach how to describe or talk about an item/object.

Gross Motor Skills
Goal: The child will be able to demonstrate age appropriate gross motor skills.
Materials: Cones or dividers set up in the backyard to resemble an obstacle course, various activities/objects for the child to engage with
Teaching Strategy: This is a fun one that older children tend to enjoy. Create an obstacle course in the child's backyard. You can use orange cones, or other dividers such as beanbags or brightly colored crates. The child should make their way through the course by running or moving very quickly, and course difficulty should be determined by the child's functioning level. For children with poor gross motor skills, the first cone could lead to a mini trampoline that they jump on 2 times, the second cone could lead to a large ball that the child tosses to you, etc. For a child with better gross motor control, you could include activities such as hanging from a bar or climbing a ladder.
Generalization: Generalize this skill by introducing sports. Mini- obstacle courses are a good way to introduce children with Autism to sports, while strengthening gross motor skills. Running back and forth between cones is good practice for

basketball, while tossing a ball to you could prepare the child for football. Decide which sport you want to focus on, and place activities in the obstacle course that resemble that sport.

> *Why is this important?* Gross motor skills are necessary to correctly manipulate a variety of items and stimuli in the environment. Gross motor refers to large muscle group actions, such as running, catching a ball, or jumping.

Grooming

Goal: The child will be able to care for their own personal hygiene including brushing teeth, washing face, combing hair, etc.

Materials: Visual strip, materials needed for specific grooming task

*Tip: Task Analysis is a technique that is helpful when teaching a skill that is really comprised of many skills or steps. Tooth brushing is a skill that to many people seems simple and straight forward, but for a child with Autism this can be a very difficult skill to learn. It is easy to create a task analysis. Just perform the skill yourself or watch someone perform the skill, and write down all of the steps. Think learning to brush teeth is pretty straight forward? Take a look at all the mini skills embedded in this task:

- Get toothbrush and toothpaste
- Wet toothbrush
- Apply toothpaste to toothbrush
- Brush upper teeth, right side of mouth
- Brush upper teeth, left side of mouth
- Brush lower teeth, right side of mouth
- Brush lower teeth, left side of mouth

- Wash mouth out with water
- Rinse off toothbrush
- Put away toothbrush and toothpaste

All of the above steps together make a task analysis. If you haven't contacted success teaching a complex skill to a child with Autism, try creating a task analysis. You may find that breaking the complex skill down and teaching one step at a time helps the child contact success.

Teaching Strategy: Create a visual strip of the grooming activity you are teaching. A visual strip is a series of photos that when placed in order, display the correct sequence of steps necessary to perform the skill. If you can, create a visual strip consisting of the child actually performing the task. Use the visual strip to help the child learn the necessary steps, and the correct order. For example, tell the child "Let's wash face". Get out the visual strip and point to each step that the child should perform: "First, wet your face. Next, get the soap. Then,……". Provide praise as the child completes each step, and gradually reduce the prompting needed from you for them to complete the task.

Generalization: Help generalize grooming skills by having the child pretend to do the skill out of the natural context. I like to do this during a game of Simon Says. For example, "Simon Says brush your teeth" or "Simon Says comb your hair". The child should imitate the grooming skill, such as pretending to brush their teeth with a toothbrush.

Why is this important? Grooming is a self help skill, which will help the child to become more independent.

From A to Z!

25

Hand Raising

Goal: The child will appropriately raise their hand in the classroom setting

Materials: Hand raising visual (could be a word or photo), mastered targets or activities

*Tip: Many children with Autism have difficulty understanding when to raise their hand, and when it isn't necessary. The hand raising visual will help distinguish with this.

Teaching Strategy: Sit down with the child 1:1 and ask them to a series of questions or activities they already know how to do (mastered targets or activities). Prompt the child to raise their hand before they answer you by holding up the hand raising visual. That would look like this:

"How old are you?" (hold up the hand raising visual)
Child raises hand, you provide praise "Good raising your hand! How old are you?"
Child responds "Six".
Provide reinforcement and praise to child.

Increase the difficulty of the skill by practicing hand raising in a 1:2 format, then 1:4, and finally in a group setting. As the child learns the skill of raising their hand, gradually remove the hand raising visual by making it smaller and smaller. Eventually you can use a reminder only before asking a question such as, "Remember to raise your hand if you want to answer".

Generalization: Hand raising is a school skill, so this skill only needs to be generalized across various teachers or classrooms by having multiple teachers or school staff use the same hand raising visual with the child.

> *Why is this important?* Hand raising is often required of children in the classroom setting and is an important educational skill.

Homework

Goal: The child will be able to independently complete homework assignments upon request.

Materials: Reinforcers, homework assignment, "Break" cards with written time increments

*Tip: Homework is a difficult and frustrating task for many children with Autism, or related special needs such as Downs Syndrome or ADHD. When dealing with a child who hates doing homework or refuses to do homework, it's important to determine what is deficit based and what is behaviorally based. A true deficit is a skill the child lacks, such as not being able to read or write well. This would cause much frustration and possibly embarrassment to the child during homework time. If the refusal to do homework is behaviorally based, that means the homework lacks reinforcement to the child, the child is using behavior to get out of the task completely, or the child has compliance issues and doesn't follow adult given commands.

Teaching Strategy: Select a few reinforcers that are motivating to the child. Create 2-5 break cards that have varying amounts of time listed on them. Prepare the homework area by choosing a quiet, minimally distracting area and making sure all homework materials are present (calculator, books, paper, etc.). Explain to the child that you are there to help them with their homework and they will be able to earn reinforcement

From A to Z!

during homework time. You can choose to reinforce appropriate behavior, correct answers, or staying on task, depending on the individual child. Place the break cards where the child can clearly see them, and explain to them that they can request a break at any time. Each break card can only be used once. The amount of time stated on the break card is how long the child can be on break, e.g. 5 minutes, 3 minutes, 1 minute, etc. Once each break has ended, be sure to bring the child immediately back to the homework area and transition them to the work task. Increase the difficulty of the skill by using fewer break cards over time, such as reducing the break cards from 5 to 2. Over time as the child learns the skill, gradually reduce the amount of time you sit by the child and offer assistance until you are just checking on the child periodically as they complete their homework.
Generalization: Generalize this skill by sharing your homework strategy with the teacher, to use in the classroom. When the child is given independent work tasks to complete in the classroom, the teacher can embed reinforcement and use time increment break cards to gain compliance.

Why is this important? Successful completion of grade level homework is an important educational skill.

Identical Matching
Goal: The child will be able to match identical objects or photos.
Materials: Two identical sets of play food
Teaching Strategy: Initiate a pretend play game with the child by pretending to cook a meal using the play food. Have the child help you "cook" by asking them to give you specific ingredients. Use bowls or containers to help the child match.

From A to Z!

28
Place one of the matches in the bowl, so the child has something to match to. For example, place an apple in a bowl and give the child the matching apple. Then tell the child to "match" by placing their apple in the bowl. Make the task fun by pretending to make a dish out of each successful match. Increase the difficulty of the skill by giving the child the correct item, as well as a non correct item. For example, give the child an apple and a lemon, and then tell them to "match" to the apple in the bowl.
Generalization: Generalize this skill by introducing non identical matching. Start with materials that are similar but different, such as a red apple and a green apple. Eventually move to items that are very dissimilar, such as a red apple and a fork.

> *Why is this important?* Identical matching is a visual performance skill that is important for learning to identify similarities of items/objects based on various characteristics such as shape or color.

Independent Play Skills
Goal: The child will be able to engage in appropriate leisure activities.
*Tip: It is common that many children with Autism lack appropriate leisure skills. When left alone and without anything to do, these children may engage in repetitive self-stimulatory behaviors or inappropriate behaviors such as climbing onto the kitchen counters. It can be incredibly helpful and beneficial to a household to teach a child with Autism to engage in appropriate leisure activities, and this also helps relieve the burden of keeping the child constantly engaged.

From A to Z!

29

Materials: 3-5 plastic boxes with lids that contain simple activities the child can easily complete, timer

Teaching Strategy: Place a different simple activity in each box, such as a picture flip-book, a puzzle, molding clay, etc. Line the boxes up and direct the child to go get a box, sit back down, open the box, complete the activity, return the activity to the box, and move to the next box. For younger children you may need to explain this sequence of steps using visuals. Use the timer to set a time limit for the child. Start slow by keeping the time short: 1 minute maximum. As the child learns the skill, increase the time. Keep the motivation to complete the tasks high by only using activities the child can easily complete. If the child struggles to complete puzzles, don't place a puzzle in one of the boxes. You can also embed reinforcement into this task by having some boxes that only contain a reinforcer, such as a box with a cookie inside. The child should open the box, eat the cookie, and then proceed to the next box. If you need to provide assistance to the child to complete this activity, try and use gestural or modeling prompting only. This will make it easier to eventually reduce your presence until the child is independently completing all of the boxes.

Generalization: Generalize this skill by increasing the amount of boxes to complete, and placing more time on the timer. Many classrooms can also easily include this activity throughout the day. Talk to the child's teacher and see if they can incorporate this strategy in the classroom, to help your child generalize this skill.

Why is this important? Independent play is a social/play skill that can also help provide appropriate leisure activities and decrease problem behaviors and/or self-stimulatory behaviors.

Initiate Greetings

Goal: The child will be able to greet others appropriately in social settings.

Materials: N/A

Teaching Strategy: It is helpful to teach initiating greetings by teaching the child to wave first. Once you have taught the child to wave in response to being waved to, shape this behavior by having the child greet the person they are waving to. Model this behavior by waving to the child as you say "Hi Lisa". Prompt the child to echo you using your name, "Hi Mommy". Start slowly by having 1 person work on the skill at a time. This is much easier than expecting the child to perform the skill for mom, dad, the babysitter, and grandma. As the child learns the skill and adds the expressive skill (greeting) to the receptive skill (waving), then you can increase the difficulty of the task by waving at the child without saying anything. Prompt the child to greet you by name as they wave at you "Hi Mommy". Once the child has greeted you, provide praise and then greet the child back "Good girl! Hi Lisa".

Generalization: Generalize this skill by using different people (inducing peers and adults) to practice the skill. Move slowly; don't begin working on generalization of other people until the child is successfully combining verbal greetings with waving. You may need to use prompting to label the person for the child ("Say hi Grace"), if it is an unknown adult or peer.

Why is this important? Greeting others is an important social skill that will help the child interact with people in their environment.

From A to Z!

Join peer play
Goal: The child will appropriately join the play of peers.
Materials: Index cards, known peers
Teaching Strategy: Choose 1-2 peers that the child is familiar with. Use the index cards to write simple statements such as "Can I play" or "My name is Corey". If the child is verbal, prompt them to say the statement on the card to the peer (or group of peers). If the child does not talk, they can give the card to the peer. You may need to prompt the other children to take the card, or to invite the child to join their play. Increase the difficulty of the skill by practicing with unknown peers, as well as known peers (with unknown peers, you may need to explain to the children beforehand to take the card and let the child play with them).
Generalization: Generalize this skill by reducing the use of the index card, which is a visual prompt. Walk over to a group of peers with the child and try a verbal prompt ("What do you say?"). If that isn't effective, then use the visual prompt (the index card).

Why is this important? The ability to join a group of peers will help a child be more social with other children.

Knocking on Doors
Goal: The child will appropriately respect a closed or locked door, by knocking before entering.
Materials: Social Story about knocking

From A to Z!

32

Teaching Strategy: A Social Story is a teaching tool often used in ABA to help teach a child about a desired behavior. A social story is a short story designed to teach a specific concept. The story should be individualized to the child, tailored to their interests, and have a specific goal (or goals) that you are trying to teach, reinforce, or generalize. It may take repeated presentations of the social story for the child to apply the information described in the story to their own life and change their own behavior. Create a social story for the child by writing a 2-3 page book about the desired behavior. Use photos of the child, and put their name into the story. A great technique to help children with Autism respond to Social Stories is to put a beloved character or person of interest in the story. Children with Autism often have cartoons, movies, or books they enjoy greatly, such as Spongebob. For a child who loves anything Spongebob related, the social story could be about how Spongebob always knocks when he visit someone's house, or he knocks before walking into his parents bedroom. Including a liked character will help grab the child's interest, and make the story more exciting. The Social Story should include what you want the child to do, instead of focusing on what they should NOT do. Use positive language and short, simple sentences. Read the story to the child regularly, and ask questions to determine their level of understanding, such as "Why did Spongebob knock on the door before he entered the house?"

Generalization: Social stories are easy to generalize, by having the child practice the skill. Be sure to read the Social Story to the child before they practice the skill. For younger children, after reading the story you can model the desired behavior for them. Take the child to visit a friend or neighbor, and prompt them to walk up to the front door and knock. Provide praise to the child for knocking, and being sure to wait for someone to open the door (Many children with Autism will knock, but then immediately turn the knob. Teach the child to knock and wait).

Why is this important? Knocking is a social skill that is considered to be good manners.

Labeling common objects

Goal: The child will be able to label common objects found in their environment

Materials: Sock, spoon

Teaching Strategy: Teach the child the name of objects in their environment by intentionally giving them objects they do not need. Prepare a bowl of cereal for the child, and instead of a spoon, place a sock next to their bowl. The child will probably look at you, push the sock away, or in some way indicate that they don't have what they need. Initially, just label the object for the child, "Oh, you don't need a sock. You need a spoon (hand the child a spoon). This is a spoon." Repeat the scenario later in the day by handing the child their shoes, a sock, and a spoon. Say to the child "What do you need? You need another sock." As the child learns the skill, instead of saying the label for the child try pausing to see if the child will say it themselves. For example "What do you need? You need a ____." Eventually require that the child requests the items they need, without you saying any statements to prompt them to ask.

Generalization: Generalize this skill by looking for opportunities to "accidentally" give the child an incorrect item or object, so the child will have to request what they need.

> *Why is this important?* The language skill of labeling, or tacting, helps a child understand that everything in their environment has a name.

Mand for Information

Goal: The child will be able to mand for information from others by asking "What's that?"

Materials: Small electronic toys that make sounds

Teaching Strategy: Sit near the child and play with the electronic toy by causing it to make sounds. Say out loud repeatedly "What's that?" If the child comes over to you to look at the toy or try to take the toy, place the toy behind your back and prompt the child to say "What's that?" Once they repeat after you they can have the toy. You may need to get very close to the child and show them the toy to spark an interest in it. Once the child shows interest, place the toy behind your back and prompt the child to ask you "What's that?" Praise the child for asking, and then label the item for them as you give them the toy.

Generalization: Generalize this skill by teaching the child's siblings or peers to walk up to the child and show them an interesting gadget or toy, and then walk away. When the child follows the other child or tries to take the object, the peer or sibling can prompt them to ask "What's that?"

> *Why is this important?* The language skill of manding helps a child understand how to request desired items or information.

Motor Imitation

Goal: The child will be able to imitate the motor actions of others.

Materials: N/A

Teaching Strategy: One of the best ways to teach motor imitation in a fun way is to play the game "Simon Says" with the child. This game of imitating helps children learn to attend, follow directions, and also to imitate the actions of another person. Start simply with just you and the child. Sit directly in front of the child (knees touching) so you can easily provide prompting if needed. Make the game fun by having the child imitate very fast or very slow, such as "Simon says wiggle your arm….FAST!" Provide praise to the child when they imitate you only after you say "Simon says". Increase the difficulty of this skill by adding in other players, or increasing the amount of distance between you and the child (such as 3 feet).

Generalization: Generalize this skill by simply saying "Do This". If you state the action you want the child to imitate, that is actually a one step instruction which isn't the same as pure imitation. Instead of saying "Simon says touch your head", say "Simon says do this!" as you touch your head. If the child does not respond or imitates incorrectly, then you can give the full prompt of "Simon says touch your head" as you physically prompt the child to touch their head.

Why is this important? Imitation is a skill that promotes learning, in a classroom setting as well as out in the community.

Making Choices

Goal: The child will be able to make choices between 2 or more items.

Materials: Reinforcers that the child enjoys

Teaching Strategy: A great way to get a child with Autism to understand choice making is to offer a *good* option and a *great* option. One way to do this is by offering "1" or "2". Gather a few reinforcers that the child really loves. Offer the reinforcers to the child several times per day, by holding out one reinforcer in one palm and two reinforcers in the other palm. Present the option to the child and say "Do you want ONE or TWO?" For very young children you may need to help them choose by immediately giving them the first choice they reach for. Reinforce the skill by saying "You picked ONE. Here you go." Some children with Autism will reach for both options if they don't understand making choices. If this happens, close your palms, wait a few seconds, and then try again. If the child will not make a choice, then you make a choice for them. If the child does not honor the choice they made (the child picked the blue cup, but then cries for the red cup) explain to them firmly that what they picked is what they get. Do not make a habit of switching items after the child made a choice, as it will only take longer for the child to understand the concept of making choices.

Generalization: Generalize this skill by including more opportunities to make choices in the child's day. Help the child learn this skill by offering obvious choices at first, such as cereal or an empty bowl. Place both items before the child and ask them "Which one do you want?" The child can

From A to Z!

receptively make a choice (point to the item) or expressively respond. As the child learns the skill, increase the difficulty by adding more choice options.

Why is this important? Making choices allows the child to have more autonomy as well as control over their environment.

Number ID

Goal: The child will be able to receptively label numbers.
Materials: Various groupings of 3-D items (e.g. buttons, pennies, socks, pebbles, marbles, etc.)
*Tip: It is often easier to teach a child to recognize numbers if the child can already count objects, or can count using their fingers. The objects or fingers can be used as a prompt if the child doesn't recognize the written number.
Teaching Strategy: Have the child count small groupings of items, such as 2 pennies, or 4 marbles. Praise the child for correctly counting the objects, being sure to provide prompting if necessary. Repeat the activity with the additional step of placing the number of objects above each pile of objects. For example, place the number 3 above a pile of 3 buttons. After the child counts the objects in each grouping, ask them to identify the number "We have 3 buttons. Point to 3." Increase the difficulty of this task by removing the grouping of items, and placing the numbers in a row of 2-3. Have the child point identify each number by touching it or pointing to it (e.g. "Point to number 5").
Generalization: Generalize this skill by using a wide variety of 3-D objects, during different parts of the day. During breakfast, have the child find the number 4 on a cereal box. During outside play, write numbers on the sidewalk using

chalk and have the child receptively label the different numbers.

> *Why is this important?* Number identification is an important pre-requisite math skill.

Name Sorting/Spelling

Goal: The child will be able to receptively spell their name, when they are given the individual letters that make up their name.

Materials: Index card with the child's name written on it, individual letter cutouts

*Tip: Matching can often be a helpful first step when teaching a skill to a child with Autism, as it helps the child understand the task visually at a low difficulty level.

Teaching Strategy: Give the child the individual letter cutouts and tell them to match each letter to spell their name. The child should place each individual letter on top of the corresponding letter on the index card. Prompting may be necessary to ensure the child matches each letter in order (its best to teach the child from the start to start matching from the first letter and go in order, as it can be difficult to remove this error later). The child should match all of the letters starting with the first letter, until they have correctly "spelled" their name. Increase the difficulty of this task by having the child assemble the individual letter cutouts next to the index card, instead of on top of it.

Generalization: Generalize this skill by using different materials. Write the child's name on a plain piece of paper, and give the child individual letter cutouts. Hold up the piece of paper and tell the child to "spell their name" or to "sort" the letters. If the child needs prompting to complete the task,

From A to Z!

allow the child to match the letters by placing them directly on the piece of paper.

> *Why is this important?* Name sorting/spelling is an important academic skill.

One step instruction

Goal: The child will comply with a request to do a simple action.

Materials: N/A

*Tip: It can be easier to teach one step instruction by initially requiring that the child imitate. Once the child is successfully imitating simple actions, then you can introduce one step instruction.

Teaching Strategy: Make a game of following directions by presenting the child with several (4-7) demands at once. Younger children especially find this fun if you present the demands in an animated voice and encourage the child to do the action quickly. For example, "Stand up-Sit down- Wave-Tap table". As you state each action, complete the action yourself so the child can watch you and imitate. If the child performs all of the actions, provide reinforcement. Increase the difficulty of this task by giving the child a simple direction to follow, but no model to imitate. Say to the child "stand up", without actually standing up yourself. If the child performs the one step instruction correctly, provide specific praise such as "Very nice standing up!".

Generalization: Generalize this skill by having different people provide one step instructions to the child, such as a family friend, sibling, or teacher. This will also help the child understand that they must comply with a variety of people, across different environments.

From A to Z!

> *Why is this important?* One step instruction helps a child learn to attend, and increases compliance.

Puzzles
Goal: The child will be able to independently complete puzzles of inset, peg, or jigsaw variety.
Materials: A simple puzzle with large pieces (For younger children, a peg style puzzle is recommended. As the child advances in their ability to complete a puzzle, move on to inset, and then jigsaw style puzzles), and a color photograph of the puzzle that is enlarged to the same size as the puzzle.
*Tip: Matching can often be a helpful first step when teaching a skill to a child with Autism, as it helps the child understand the task visually at a low difficulty level.
Teaching Strategy: Take a photo of the complete puzzle, and print it out so that it is in color and the same size as the puzzle. Place the picture on a flat surface and give the child 1-2 puzzle pieces. Tell the child to match the puzzle pieces by placing them on top of the picture. Gradually add in more puzzle pieces until the child can match more and more of the puzzle. Children complete puzzles in a variety of ways. The child might seem to have a trial and error approach, or they may work from left to right, or bottom to top. What's most important is that the child understands to look at pieces carefully and determine which piece should go where and how to make pieces "fit" together. Increase the difficulty of this task by removing the color photograph, and having the child complete the puzzle as designed. You can also increase the difficulty level by using smaller puzzle pieces, or a puzzle

that is less colorful and more monochromatic (such as a blue sky with a few clouds).

Generalization: Generalize the skill of completing puzzles by having the child work on a variety of puzzle types and sizes. Vary between inset, jigsaw, and peg puzzles. Some children with Autism may become very particular about how the puzzle must be completed. It is good to vary how the puzzle must be completed to avoid this rigidity. For example, hand the child a puzzle to complete but you put in the first 2 pieces.

Why is this important? Completing puzzles is a visual performance skill, and also teaches the child a play skill which can help with social interaction.

Prepositions

Goal: The child will understand the concept of prepositions.
Materials: 3-D worm, small box with a lid
*Tip: If you are having difficulty teaching a specific concept to a child with Autism, it can be very helpful to make the task more visual so the child can "see" the task instead of having to rely on cognitive processes to understand the task.
Teaching Strategy: Make this activity fun by giving the worm a name, such as "Danny". Give the child the 3-D worm and place the box in front of the child. Tell the child to place Danny in various positions such as above, below, or inside of the box. Provide prompting as necessary. Encourage the child to have Danny crawl from place to place. For verbal children, reinforce the skill by asking them to expressively identify the preposition. For example "Put Danny **inside** the box. Nice job! Where is Danny? He's **inside** the box." Increase the difficulty of the skill by taking Danny out into the community and have

the child place Danny in various positions, such as **next to** the stop sign, **under** the chair, **inside** the grocery cart, etc. Generalization: Generalize this skill by removing the 3-D worm and having the child perform the task. Tell the child "sit **under** the chair", or "stand **on top** of the table". Use the worm to help prompt if necessary, such as placing the worm under the chair first and then telling the child "sit under the chair".

Why is this important? Understanding prepositions is an important academic skill.

Phone Number

Goal: The child will be able to state their telephone number when asked to do so.
Materials: Visual of the telephone number
*Tip: When teaching expressive language, it can often be helpful to put the word, phrase, or sentence to music. This often helps children with Autism remember phrasing and pauses, such as where to leave pauses when reciting their telephone number.
Teaching Strategy: Ask the child "What's your telephone number?", and prompt them to respond in a song-song voice, or to the tune of a simple nursery rhyme. It is important to teach the child to pause correctly when stating their phone number (e.g. 111-pause-222-pause-3333). If you reinforce the child even though they run all the numbers together or are hard to understand, this can be a hard error to correct later on. For younger children, it may be helpful to use a visual of the telephone number. Ask the child "What's your telephone number?" Prompt the child to say each number by pointing to the number on the visual, and singing the number at a slightly slow pace (e.g. 111....-pause-222....-pause-3333).

43

Generalization: Generalize the skill by varying slightly the way you ask the question. Such as, "Tell me your phone number" and "Hey, what is your telephone number?" This will ensure that even if someone asks the child using different wording, the child will still be able to state their telephone number.

> *Why is this important?* Knowing safety information (such as your telephone number) is important for children in the case of an emergency.

Quiet Hands

Goal: The child will keep hands still and calm during instruction time.

Materials: Construction paper, contact paper or laminate

*Tip: When working with a child with Autism 1:1 (even if the child is very young), it's important that the child knows how to calm their body for instruction. This would include sitting up straight in their chair, eyes on the teacher or therapist, and their mouth, hands, and feet should be quiet, calm, and still. Even very young, pre-school aged children need to know how to display these attending behaviors.

Teaching Strategy: Have the child place their hands flat on the construction paper, and trace a thick outline around the child's hands. Cut out the outline of the child's hands, and laminate the hands or use contact paper to attach them to the desk or table where instruction happens. This provides the child with a visual prompt of where there hands should be during instruction. During instruction, if the child begins to grab or stim on materials or becomes fidgety/off task, say to the child "quiet hands" and prompt them to place their hands directly on top of the hand visuals. For older children, it may be more appropriate to use a smaller visual, such as 2 small stickers on the desk (they would place their hands on top of the stickers), or an index card that says "Quiet hands". Generalization: Generalize this skill by teaching the child how to have quiet hands outside of instructional time, and away from a worktable or desk. Teach the child that folding their hands can also be considered "quiet hands", and is an appropriate response. Teach this by modeling the behavior for the child, by saying "quiet hands" and then folding your own hands.

Why is this important? Children who cannot properly calm their bodies to attend during instruction time may miss important learning opportunities.

Reading

Goal: The child will be able to read simple words.
Materials: Small photo album, various labeled pictures
*Tip: Begin to teach reading by having the child "read" photos before reading words.
Teaching Strategy: Get a small photo album with plastic sleeves. Make a list of objects that the child can label. For each object, create a label and a photo. Such as a picture of a cupcake with the word "cupcake" at the bottom. Create a simple picture book, with a story involving the objects the child can label. As you read the book to the child, point to the photos of the objects the child knows and then pause and wait for the child to label the item. Over time, remove the photo of

45

the object and just have the word. Use your finger on the page as a guide to help the child read from left to right, and top to bottom.

Generalization: Generalize this skill by revising the picture book to include objects the child does not currently know. Help the child to decode the unknown words by sounding the word out phonetically. The child will also enjoy having a picture book that changes from time to time.

Why is this important? Reading is an important academic skill.

Responding to Name

Goal: The child will respond to their name being called by giving eye contact.

Materials: N/A

Teaching Strategy: It is often necessary to teach young children to look when their name is called by modifying what happens if they do not look. Teach the child to respond with eye contact to their name by using reinforcement. Place a few small reinforcers in your pocket, such as cookies or pretzel pieces. Walk up to the child and call their name. If the child does not look at you, hold up a reinforcer next to your eyes, get in the child's direct line of sight (squat or stoop, if needed), and call their name again. When the child looks at you, provide specific praise ("Thank you for looking at me") and give the child the reinforcer. If the child looks at the reinforcer and not at you, move the reinforcer closer to your eyes. Over time, the child will be more likely to look at people when they hear their name called because it has been repeatedly linked to reinforcement. Do not provide access to the reinforcer if the child will not look at you, but use prompting to gain eye contact (such as turning the child's face toward you).

From A to Z!

46

Generalization: Generalize this skill by gradually placing more distance between you and the child. Stand 1 foot away from the child and call their name, then 2 feet, etc.

> *Why is this important?* Responding to name is a very important skill to teach children with Autism, who can respond to their name so rarely that they may appear to be hard of hearing.

Sequencing

Goal: The child will be able to understand the concept of order or sequencing, such as first to last, or 1st, 2nd, 3rd, etc

Materials: Create a visual schedule of a simple chore, such as setting the table. Include a photo of each step needed to set the table. Label the first photo "first", the next photo "second", and so on

*Tip: When teaching abstract concepts to a child with Autism, try to make the task more concrete by making it specific to an activity the child does regularly.

Teaching Strategy: Tell the child to perform the chore (e.g. "Set the table"). Hold up the visual to remind the child each step to complete, and provide verbal reminders of the order of steps. For example "What do you do first? That's right, plates on table. Then what? Awesome, cups on table." Verbally direct the child through each step, in the correct order. If the child attempts to complete steps out of order, or becomes "lost" in the middle of the chore, use prompting and the visual schedule to remind them what step they are on, and what comes next. Increase the difficulty of this task by minimizing your verbal feedback and asking the child to tell you each step, e.g. "What comes first?" As the child's

understanding of sequencing increases, modify the visual schedule to include more language and less photos.
Generalization: Generalize this skill by practicing sequencing steps on a variety of tasks throughout the day, such as making a meal, doing laundry, brushing teeth, washing dishes, etc.
Why is this important? Sequencing/making patterns is a visual performance skill, and also a pre-requisite math skill.

Speaking slowly
Goal: The child will speak at an appropriate and intelligible speed.
Materials: Visual of a cheetah and a turtle
Teaching Strategy: When the child talks too fast and runs their words together, tell them you can't understand because it's "too fast". Hold up the visual of the cheetah to help the child understand. It may be helpful to talk about how cheetahs run very fast, and fast is good for running but not so good for talking. Model for the child how you want them to speak, and tell them to try again. It's important not to reinforce unintelligible, garbled speech that is too fast. If the child requests a cookie by speaking very quickly and is hard to understand, then do not give them the cookie until they slow down and ask you again. Reinforce the child for using appropriate speed of speech. When the child speaks appropriately, hold up the visual of the turtle and provide praise. It may be helpful to talk about how the turtle moves very slowly, and when the turtle speaks he is very easy to understand.
Generalization: Generalize this skill by placing the visuals where the child can see them, but not holding up the visuals and explaining what the child should do. Only refer to the

visuals as needed, such as pointing to the cheetah and asking the child to "say it slow". Gradually fade out the visuals, until you can just prompt the child to "say it slow".

Why is this important? It is important for social interaction that other people can understand the child's speech, and words.

Sweeping

Goal: The child will be able to independently sweep a floor.
Materials: Child-sized broom and dustpan
*Tip: Imitation is a very helpful tool when teaching children with Autism a self help skill. It is much easier to imitate a skill than to complete it independently.
Teaching Strategy: Have the child observe you sweeping a floor and then have the child stand next to you and imitate the action of sweeping (without holding anything). As you sweep the floor, say to the child "Show me sweeping". Once the child can pretend to sweep, hand the child a child sized broom and dustpan and have them imitate you using the objects. Use prompting to help the child sweep up dirt and use a proper 2 hand grip on the broom.
Generalization: Generalize this skill by increasing the distance between you and the child (sweep 1 foot, then 2 feet, then 3 feet away from the child) until you can watch the child sweep independently and they no longer need a model to imitate.

Why is this important? Sweeping is a household chore that can help make the child more independent, and also an adaptive skill.

Telling jokes

Goal: The child will be able to understand the concept of telling a joke, or making a humorous statement.

Materials: Flashcards

*Tip: When teaching older children with Autism to tell jokes, it can be very helpful to observe how typically developing children tell jokes and what they find funny.

Teaching Strategy: Place a few flashcards inside a paper bag, and have the child pull out 2 cards. Then you pull out 2 cards. Take turns telling simple knock- knock jokes based on what's on each flashcard. This may require much prompting at first depending on the functioning level of the child. Help the child understand what humorous statements are. For some older children, teaching them about "nonsense" statements or things that don't make sense is a good introduction to humor. Such as picturing a cow driving a car, or a fish wearing glasses. Provide socially appropriate praise (lots of laughter!) to the child's joke telling attempts, and then model appropriate joke telling for the child. Increase the difficulty of the task by having the child tell jokes to various people, including both adults and peers.

Generalization: Generalize this skill by moving away from the flashcards, and helping the child generate ideas about what to make a joke about.

Why is this important? Joke telling is a complex social skill that will help the child interact with people in their environment.

Turn Taking

Goal: The child will be able to appropriately take turns and display the ability to share.

From A to Z!

50

Materials: Easel, 2 containers paint, 2 paintbrushes

*Tip: It is easier to teach turn taking initially by "joining in" the child's play or activity, rather than by taking something from the child.

*Tip: Some children with Autism struggle to understand pronouns ("my turn/your turn"). If you want to avoid using pronouns then just replace "my/your" with names. For example, "Mommy's turn/Claire's turn". For younger children it may be helpful to point to them when it's their turn and point to yourself when it's your turn.

Teaching Strategy: Slowly desensitize the child to turn taking by gradually requiring more and more sharing of objects. Set up an easel, and have the child pick which color they want to paint with. Select your own paint, and then begin to paint next to the child, with each of you using your own painting supplies. Next, tell the child you are going to share their paint color by saying "my turn" as you dip your paintbrush in their paint (Do not ask the child if it is your turn because that gives the child the option of saying "no"). Continue painting, and then tell the child you are going to share their paintbrush by taking their brush and saying "my turn". It is important to keep the item only a few seconds after saying "my turn", and to say "your turn" when giving the item back to the child. This helps the child understand that even when you take an item, you will give it back. As the child seems to understand the concept of turn taking, you can hold your hand out and say "my turn" instead of just taking the item. Also practice keeping the item for longer periods of time. If the child tries to take the item back from you, use blocking and repeat "It's my turn". Increase the difficulty of this skill by only using one set of materials to paint: 1 easel, 1 container of paint, 1 paintbrush. When you say "my turn", then it is your turn to paint and you are the only one who can paint at that time. When you say "your turn", then the child should be the only one painting.

Generalization: Generalize this skill by having the child practice turn taking with another peer. Children with Autism will often interact or share with an adult, but will struggle to interact and take turns with another child.

Why is this important? Turn taking is a social skill that will help the child interact with people in their environment.

Using utensils

Goal: The child will correctly use a fork or spoon during meals.

Materials: Utensils, pretend food, doll

*Tip: It is easier to teach proper use of utensils if the child gets many opportunities each day to practice. Try to prepare multiple meals each day that require the use of a fork or spoon.

Teaching Strategy: Encourage the child to feed pretend food to a babydoll using utensils (play utensils or real utensils are fine). Hand the child a pretend piece of cake and a fork and tell them to "feed the baby". Use hand over hand prompting to help the child grip the utensil correctly. Use a variety of pretend foods that require stabbing (fork) or scooping (spoon). Provide praise to the child for using the utensils correctly, and for younger children modeling may be helpful. Hold your own babydoll and model the correct way to feed the baby using a fork or spoon.

Generalization: Generalize this skill by having the child use utensils at meal times, and prompt them to avoid using their fingers and to use a fork or spoon instead.

> *Why is this important?* Using utensils appropriately is a self help skill, which will help the child to become more independent.

Vocal Imitation

Goal: Teach the child to vocally imitate the words or sounds of someone else.

Materials: A toy microphone, music

*Tip: Using a microphone makes emitting language more fun for the child. There is the auditory stimulation from the echo of the microphone, the tactile stimulation of getting to hold the microphone, or the tactile stimulation of feeling the vibration of the microphone against their mouth or lips

Teaching Strategy: Play some music and have fun singing songs into a toy microphone. Watch the child's reaction to see which songs they like, by seeing if they clap, dance, or smile. During one of the child's favorite songs, pause the music and place the microphone to the child's mouth. If necessary, you can prompt the child by saying "You sing!" If the child makes any sound (its important to reinforce even the slightest sound) provide huge praise and reinforcement, and continue singing songs and playing music. As the child learns that they are supposed to "sing" when it is their turn, make this skill more difficult by giving the child a specific sound or word to imitate. For example, pause the music and hold the microphone up to the child's mouth and say "Say MMMMMM".

Generalization: You can generalize this skill by playing the child's favorite songs in the car, and seeing if you can get the child to sing along with you without the microphone present. Play the music loudly and sing animatedly, and then pause the music and see if the child will continue singing by themselves (see if the child will "fill in" the missing music). If the child does, be sure to provide huge praise.

Why is this important? Being able to vocally imitate will make language acquisition more successful for the child.

Walking with a Group

Goal: When in a group of people, the child will be able to stay with the group without wandering off on their own.
Materials: N/A
*Tip: This may be easier to teach if you practice "Follow the Leader" 1:1 in the home setting first.
Teaching Strategy: Prime the child before going out with a group that they must stay with the group at all times and cannot go off on their own. Tell the child they need to "Follow the Leader". Prompt the child to follow you for a few steps, and then provide reinforcement and praise (have someone else in the group stay behind the child to help the child follow you correctly). Use the other people in the group to help prompt the child to follow the leader correctly. During the outing, continue to remind the child that you are the leader and they need to follow you.
Generalization: Generalize this skill by having various people in the group be the "Leader". Tell the child who the leader is, and help them to follow that person closely and pay attention to where that person is going. If the Leader stops walking, then the child should stop walking too. As the Leader you can make this activity fun by walking very slowly, very quickly, or doing lots of starts and stops. Provide praise to the child for matching your speed and staying with you.

> *Why is this important?* Staying with a group in public is a social skill that will help the child interact with people in their environment, and can also help maintain safety.

Writing Letters

Goal: The child will be able to correctly write letters.
Materials: Container or box of sand, individual letter cut-outs
*Tip: It can be helpful to teach children with Autism to write by breaking up the complex skill of writing into: forming letters correctly, and using writing utensils correctly. This activity focuses on forming letters correctly into sand, which is much easier than gripping a pen or pencil.
Teaching Strategy: Place a container of sand in front of the child and have them form different letters by using their fingers to "write" on the sand. For younger children, use modeling to help the child form letters. It may take much repetition for the child to learn the correct form of each letter.
Generalization: Generalize this skill by having the child write in a typical manner, using a pen/pencil and paper. If prompting is necessary, have the child "write" the letter in the sand using a writing utensil (instead of their finger), and then have them write on paper.

> *Why is this important?* Handwriting is an important academic skill.

Waiting

Goal: The child will be able to wait appropriately to start or stop a task, or to access a desired item.

From A to Z!

55

Materials: Clear container that has a lid

*Tip: Allowing the child to see the item they are waiting for can help to lessen the anxiety reaction that children with Autism may exhibit when told to wait.

Teaching Strategy: When the child requests (either expressively or receptively) a specific item or object, place the item inside of the container, close the lid, and tell the child to "Wait". Practice this multiple times throughout the day, and be sure to provide praise when the child waits nicely to access the desired item. For younger children, it may be helpful to count out loud or use a visual timer to help the child understand the passage of time. Increase the difficulty of the task by having the child wait for longer periods of time, such as several minutes. For example, if the child must wait to drink juice until they have finished their snack, then place the juice inside of a clear container next to the child's plate. Once the child has finished their snack, open the container and give them the juice. Be sure to provide specific praise such as "That was nice waiting! Here is your juice".

Generalization: Generalize this skill by also having the child wait to access activities, such as waiting 10 seconds to enter the playroom. Before providing access to an activity, stop at the entrance of it and say to the child "wait". The child must wait nicely and quietly for the full duration of time before they can access the activity.

Why is this important? **The ability to wait is a social skill that will help the child interact with people in their environment, and is also necessary to be successful in the classroom.**

Xylophone to teach patterns

Goal: The child will be able to imitate a simple sequence, or pattern, of colors using a xylophone.

Materials: Xylophone

*Tip: For younger children, keep a simple pattern design such as 1-3 colors. For older children, they may enjoy more complex patterns with multiple colors.

Teaching Strategy: Sit with the child and begin to play with a xylophone toy. Create a simple color pattern for the child to imitate ("Do This"), such as hitting green and then yellow. Then hand the child the xylophone and prompt them to hit green, and then yellow. The child should watch closely to see which keys you tap on the xylophone, and should then imitate the color pattern you created. Increase the difficulty of this task by moving away from imitation. Create a simple color pattern, such as red-blue-red-blue. Then stop and ask the child what comes next. The child can answer "red", or they can hit the red key on the xylophone.

Generalization: Generalize this skill by doing this activity on a keyboard on a piano, and having the child imitate a sound sequence. Begin very simply with a 1-2 note pattern, and as the child learns the skills move to a sound pattern that is several notes long.

Why is this important? Pattern making is a visual performance skill, and also a pre-requisite math skill to understand why things work together.

57
Yes/No questions

Goal: The child will be able to correctly respond to "yes" or "no" questions.

Materials: N/A

*Tip: Answering yes/no questions can be a hard skill for children with Autism to learn. It is common that the child may learn to answer "no" when they do not want something, but when they do want something instead of saying "yes" they may engage in echolalia (e.g. Adult: "Do you want some juice?" Child: "Juice").

Teaching Strategy: Wait for the child to make a request, such as "I want water" or "Milk please". Once you know what the child wants, turn their request into a question. Ask the child "Do you want water?" or "Do you want milk?", and prompt the child to respond with a "yes" or "no". This should make it easier for the child to answer with a "yes" or "no", because they have already stated they want the item. For younger children, it may be helpful to hold out the item in front of the child as a reminder of what they want. Ask the child "Do you want water?", as you hold the cup of water out to them. Do not allow the child to access the desired item until they answer your question. Once the child says "yes", then they can have the desired item. Be sure to provide praise and reinforcement when the child responds with a "yes" or "no". For children who do not talk, they can nod their head to indicate "yes" or shake their head to indicate "no".

Generalization: Generalize this task by asking the child more challenging "yes" or "no" questions, such as characteristics of objects. For example, ask the child "Is this food" as you hold up a shoe. Or point to the child's mother and ask "Is that Daddy?"

> *Why is this important?* Answering "yes" or "no" questions will allow other people to verbally communicate with the child, and foster social skill development.

Zipping up/ down

Goal: The child will be able to independently use a zipper.
Materials: Adult size zip up jacket
*Tip: It's often easier to teach a child with Autism to learn to use a zipper if the zipper is not on the child's person. Most people teach children to zip using their pants or clothing, but for a child with Autism who may have difficulty attending or looking at the zipper, its much easier if the zipper is separate from their body. When transitioning from a zipper off the body to one on the body, you may need to repeatedly remind the child to look at the zipper as they zip up or down.
Teaching Strategy: Give the child an adult sized jacket, or wrap the jacket around a chair or pillow. Tell the child to zip up/down. Prompt the child to use 2 hands to zip up or down as they keep their gaze on the zipper. It can be helpful to start with zipping down, as many children struggle with beginning a proper zip up. Increase the difficulty of this skill by using a child sized jacket, with a smaller zipper.
Generalization: Generalize this task by having the child first perform the task using a piece of clothing, and then put the clothing on the child and have them perform the task. For example, have the child zip down Daddy's jacket. Then place the jacket on the child and have them zip up Daddy's jacket.

> *Why is this important?* Correctly using a zipper is a self help skill which will help the child be more independent.

Glossary of Terms

Adaptive skill- Adaptive skills consist of various life skills important for meaningful interaction with society, such as hygiene, meal preparation, dressing oneself, etc.

Behavioral trigger- A behavioral trigger is any event (internal or external) that serve as the motivation for a problem behavior to occur. Examples include being hungry, lack of sleep, or excessive noise.

Compliance- Compliance refers to following directions or instructions.

Echolalia- Echolalia is repeating the words of another person, such as a child saying "Hi Julie" when an adult says to the child "Hi Julie".

Expressive- Expressive refers to vocal behavior, such as talking.

Functioning level- Functioning levels are typically determined by looking at the individual's ability to communicate, engage in social interactions, and care for themselves. Functioning can range from very high, to very low.

Generalization/generalize- (see Generalization: What is It)

Hand over hand prompting (HOH) - HOH prompting means to physically place your hand over the child's hand and move their hand to complete the desired response.

Mand- A mand is a verbal operant that refers to requesting, such as a child asking for food because they are hungry.

Meltdown- A meltdown goes far beyond a tantrum, and is depicted by a loss of control, lack of concern for ones own safety, and an inability to calm down.

Pincer grip- The pincer grip is the grasp used by the thumb and index finger to pick up or hold items.

Praise- (see Praise Jar)

Prompting- (see Prompting 101)

Receptive- Receptive refers to non vocal behavior, such as pointing or gesturing.

Reinforcement- Reinforcement is anything that increases the likelihood that a behavior will occur. Reinforcement is varied, and can include social (praise), tangible (a toy), or edible (cookie) types of reinforcement.

Self-stimulatory behaviors- Self stimulatory behavior refers to repetitive (and sometimes perplexing) behaviors that many individuals with Autism engage in. Examples include rocking, making sounds or humming, and hand flapping.

Tacting- A tact is a verbal operant that refers to labeling, such as a child seeing a car go by and saying "car".

Praise Jar

Praise is a type of reinforcement that follows the occurrence of a desirable behavior. You can use praise to reinforce behaviors you want to see occur more frequently, such as completing homework, doing chores, or saying "please" and "thank you". Many parents and professionals are aware of the power of praise and know that it can strengthen behavior, but I have found that most people don't rely on praise as much as they should.

When delivering reinforcement it is always a goal to move from tangible reinforcement (such as handing the child a piece of gum) and move toward social, intangible praise (such as compliments). There are many reasons for this, but the main reason is that in society it is much more likely that the child will access intangible praise than tangible rewards. For example, if a middle school student answers a question correctly in class, how does the teacher respond? The teacher will probably say something like "Nice job", or "That's correct!" It's unlikely that the teacher would hand the child a cookie or give them a sip of juice.
When working with children with Autism its important to always think ahead. One way to think ahead is to ensure that the reinforcement you deliver is the kind of reinforcement the child is likely to contact out in the world.

A great technique for understanding just how often and easily praise should be delivered is to create a praise jar. You will need a clear jar, and many small slips of paper. On each slip of paper write a different praise statement. Examples include:

63

"Fantastic", "Beautiful working", "Super", "Wonderful", "Outstanding", and "You're working so hard". Place the slips of paper into the jar. The goal is to empty the jar by the end of each day. Depending on the child, you may empty the jar by lunchtime. For other children, it may take all day to empty the jar. Sometimes as parents and professionals you will have to "catch the child being good", or it will be difficult to have something to praise. Look for occurrences of desirable behaviors, no matter how small. Did the child put on their shoes independently? Praise that! Did the child sit next to their brother with quiet hands and no hitting? Praise that! The point of this activity is to get into the habit of delivering praise all day long across settings and environments.

Praise can be a powerful teaching tool. It is a type of reinforcement, which means it strengthens learning. Praise can also help to build a relationship with the child, and make it easier to get the child to comply with you. For best teaching results, get in the habit of delivering varied praise on a consistent basis.

Prompting 101

A prompt is any type of cue or assistance given to encourage a desired response from an individual. Prompts are often categorized into a prompt hierarchy depending on how intrusive the prompt is. Prompts are a necessary component of ABA, and help a child move from being completely unable to do a skill, to doing that same skill independently. The goal of teaching using prompts is always to fade prompts towards independence (as much as is possible). The way you fade prompts will depend on the skill level of the child. For certain skills, the child may continue to need occasional prompting, such as a verbal reminder. When fading prompts reduce the prompt to the level where the child can be as independent as possible.

When a new skill is being introduced it is ideal to use more prompting so the child has no opportunity to get the answer wrong. Errors can impede learning as well as lead to frustration or annoyance. However if the skill is known, or the child has been working on the skill for some time, use less intrusive prompts to help the child be successful and to avoid prompt dependency. The less we help our kids, the more they are doing on their own.

Prompting Hierarchy
(In order from least to most intrusive prompting. This is not an exhaustive list of all possible prompts; it is simply a way to understand how intrusive various types of prompts are)

- **Visual prompt- a visual cue or picture**

- Modeling- performing the action you want the child to perform
- Positional- moving the target item closer to the child
- Gestural- using a physical gesture (a point, tap, touch) to indicate the correct item
- Partial Verbal prompts- saying the beginning sound of the target response ("Ba" to get the response of "Ball")
- Full Verbal prompts: saying the entire target response ("Ball" to get the response of "Ball")
- Partial Physical prompts- Using small or abbreviated physical movements to make the child select the correct response, such as tapping their elbow or hand
- Full Physical prompts: Completely physically manipulating the child to produce the correct response, such as HOH (hand over hand) prompting.

Skill Generalization: What is It?

Research has shown that children with Autism often have significant difficulty transferring skills learned in one environment to another environment (Stokes, T. F., & Baer, D. M. 1977). When teaching children with Autism it is critical to include systems of generalization in your teaching strategy. Otherwise you will have a child who can sing the alphabet song at school during Circle Time but can't recite the alphabet at grandma's house.

Unlike typically developing children, a child with Autism may not be able to apply something learned in one setting/environment to a new setting/environment. Or the child may engage in the desired skill for a short time, and then seem to lose the skill. As parents and professionals it is our job to teach in such a way that generalization of skills learned is always a priority. Just because the child can exhibit a skill in a 1:1 teaching environment, does not mean that the child will be able to exhibit that same skill at the grocery store, or on the playground. This is sometimes referred to as a lack of "functional use" of skills learned. For example, the child has learned to identify the color blue on a flashcard, but this skill does not transfer to blue cars, blue socks, blue candy, etc.

Methods to teach for generalization can include:

- Stimuli generalization- vary the materials used to teach

- Response generalization- vary the desired response from the child
- Setting generalization- vary where you teach, including time of day
- Generalization across people- vary who teaches the child

References

http://thegraycenter.org/social-stories/what-are-social-stories

http://www.autism-help.org/behavior-positive-reinforcement-autism.htm

Lovaas, O.I. (1987) "Behavioral treatment and normal educational and intellectual functioning in young autistic children," Journal *of Consulting and Clinical Psychology, 55,* 3-9

Maurice, Catherine, Green, Gina & Luce, Stephen C. (1996). *Behavioral intervention for young children with autism – A manual for parents and professionals.* Pro-Ed

Partington, J. W., & Sundberg, M. L. (1998). *Assessment of basic language and learning skills (The ABLLS): Instruction and IEP guide.*
Pleasant Hill, CA: Behavior Analysts, Inc.

R.L. Koegel & L.K. Koegel (Eds.), *Teaching children with autism: Strategies for initiating positive interactions and improving learning opportunities.* Baltimore, MD: Paul H. Brookes Publishing Co.

Stokes, T. F., & Baer, D. M. (1977). An implicit technology of generalization. Journal of Applied Behavior Analysis, 10, 349-367

Sundberg, M. L., & Partington, J.W. (1998). *Teaching language to children with autism or other developmental disabilities.* Danville, CA: Behavior Analysts, Inc.

Made in the USA
Lexington, KY
21 February 2013